Music by Elena Lange
Words by Glyn Maxwell

www.thelionsface.com

**First performance of The Lion's Face
at Theatre Royal Brighton, Brighton Festival on 20 May 2010.**

Performances 2010

20, 21 May	Theatre Royal Brighton *(Brighton Festival)*
23 May	Oxford Playhouse
25, 26 May	Northern Stage, Newcastle
28, 29 May	Watford Palace Theatre
13 July	Royal Welsh College of Music & Drama, Cardiff
16 July	Parabola Theatre, Cheltenham Ladies College *(Cheltenham Festival of Music)*
20, 21, 28, 29 July	Linbury Studio, Royal Opera House, London

For tour information visit www.thelionsface.com

Running time about 1 hour 45 mins including interval.

Welcome to The Lion's Face.

The first performance of a new opera marks the end of a long journey - and also the start of many new journeys as a work finds new meaning in the minds of an audience.

Elena Langer and Glyn Maxwell first began developing *The Lion's Face* with us almost four years ago, and there is one collaboration which has inspired us all throughout this long gestation – with Professor Simon Lovestone and his team at King's College London/Institute of Psychiatry. Their research work as well as their clinical and community work has humbled us, inspired us and allowed us to glimpse something beyond ourselves.

There have been other collaborations as well – with the artists who contributed in developmental workshops; between the science and arts funders who have made the opera possible; with the schools and their local theatres working with us on workshops linking music and dementia; with the local partners such as universities and hospitals who are working with their local theatres to support the opera and curate additional activity around these performances.

If this is the first time you've seen The Opera Group we hope you'll want to find out more about us. Join our mailing list and stay in touch with updates about forthcoming shows. If you are one of our regular supporters, we hope you'll find something new and surprising this time around.

We'd be very interested in your feedback on the performance or any of the surrounding activity. Please get in touch with us at enquiries@theoperagroup.co.uk or call 020 7922 2846.

John Fulljames

John Fulljames
Artistic Director

The Lion's Face was made with the generous support of:

CALOUSTE GULBENKIAN FOUNDATION, JERWOOD SPACE, THE RVW TRUST

THE LION'S FACE

Music by Elena Langer
Words by Glyn Maxwell

COMPANY

Mr. D	Dave Hill
Mrs. D	Elizabeth Sikora
Caregiver	Rachel Hynes
Caregiver's Daughter	Fflur Wyn
Clinician-Scientist	Benedict Nelson
Boy	Harry Bradford / Jonathan Bircumshaw

THE OPERA GROUP ENSEMBLE

Violin 1	Marcus Barcham-Stevens
Violin 2	Neil McTaggart
Viola	Max Baillie
Cello	Sarah Suckling
Bass	Elena Hull
Flute	Alison Hayhurst
Clarinet	Niall Webb
Oboe	James Beatty
Bassoon	Alice Lee
Trombone	Neill Hadden
Percussion	Tim Palmer
Piano	Ouri Bronchti
Conductor	Nicholas Collon
Director	John Fulljames
Designer	Alex Lowde
Lighting	Jon Clark
Projection	Ian Galloway
Sound	Fergus O'Hare
Repetiteurs	Ouri Bronchti, James Longford
Assistant Director	Lucy Bradley
Casting Consultants	Sam Jones, Sarah Playfair

Public Engagement Consultants	Paula Hamilton, Elaine Snell
Education Project Coordinator	Nina Swann
Education Artist	Pete Letanka
Evaluation	Jane Macnaughton (Co-director) and Karen Scott, Centre for Medical Humanities and David Fuller, Department of English Studies, Durham University

Production Manager	Bob Holmes
Company Stage Manager	Rupert Carlile
Deputy Stage Manager	Jennifer Llewellyn
Costume Supervisor	Johanna Coe
Technical Stage Manager	Charles Ash
Tour Lighting	Sally Ferguson
Projection Technician	Salvador Avila
Wardrobe Manager	Morag Hood
Production Photographer	Alastair Muir
Set built by	Watford Palace Theatre

FILM

Children	Dilys Childs, Octavia Coe, Lydia Coe, Zoe Hall-Zschenderlein, Martha Stutchbury, Florence Evans Thomas, Joshua Bruell, Louis Davie, Gabriel Bellamy Plaice
Art Director	Colin Falconer
Art Department Assistant	Maeve Keeley
Film Crew	Mike Kovacs, Alex Leach, Chris Stephens

Additional Thanks

Carol Rowlands, Leonie Macdonald, Julian Forsyth, David Calder, Elena Ferrari, Simon Lobelson, Richard Robinson, Cecilia Bravo, Young Vic, Tim Murray, Amy Bere, Gus Christie, Freya Wynn-Jones, Glyndebourne, Brighton Pier, Omar Shahryar, Rhona McKail, James Barralet, Michael Atkinson, Pip Donaghy, Lindy Tennent-Brown, Rachel Nicholls, Patrick Bailey and Nate Sence

Irene Brunskill, DeNDRoN, Ursula Crickmay and the Music For Life Team, Roz Finn and Haydn Stride at Longhill High School in Rottingdean, Dr Dennis Chan and the Brighton and Sussex Medical School, Catherine Turner and Lorraine Wright at Francis Coombe Academy in Watford, Dr Fourie and Dr Townel at Prospect House in Watford, Doctor Dennis Chan, Professor Gordon Wilcock, Megan Pritchard, Sarah Cant

The Lion's Face – Writing an Opera about Dementia

All a writer's work, whether poem, novel, play, screenplay, libretto, sits somewhere on a spectrum between a piece of pure imagination that cannot be researched and a piece drawn from the passing world that can *only* be researched. *The Lion's Face* sits right at the latter end of this spectrum. Of course Lena and I have applied as much musical and literary imagination to the subject as is natural and compulsive for us to do, but we both felt from the start that an operatic exploration of dementia called for a profoundly matter-of-fact engagement with the worlds touched by this still incurable disease.

Over the last five years, as the piece grew in size and scope – and with the generous and invaluable assistance of Professor Simon Lovestone and his team at the Institute of Psychiatry – we embarked upon a process of absorbing what we could through any means at our disposal, from reading, conversation with scientists and clinicians, observation of laboratory work (everything from chromatography, x-rays and brain-scans to the indefatigably helpful fruit-fly); we met carers, nurses, psychotherapists, drama and music therapists; we met people delighted we were writing an opera, we met people affronted by the notion; and, of course, we encountered some in the early stages of the disease, people still able and willing to tell us how it goes and what is does. We met some of the loved ones, the spouses and children – the oft-forgotten victims of dementia, who remain, throughout, fully aware that their lives are altering for the worse, that those they love are vanishing forever while still sitting there. This journey has been at times harrowing, at times bewildering, but also enthralling, life-affirming, funny, sweet.

Somewhere in the early stages, we hit upon the idea of making the patient, the client (the *sufferer* – the polite euphemisms can mist things up a bit) a spoken role, with the other characters singing. I think this gave us important momentum. To have one isolated speaking voice calling out in a world of song seemed a valid metaphor for the gulf between sufferer and stranger (remember: with this affliction *everyone* turns to a stranger) and it helped to make his words, his thread of English, seem helpless, frail, arbitrary, as if he were the last speaker of a dying language, which, in a way, he is.

Out of our long walk through the landscape of dementia has emerged the simple story of a chance encounter between an old man and a little girl. In a perfect world, Mr D shouldn't be there. He should not have lost the ability to recognise his wife, his sons. His words should still make sense to those around him. He should be at home, not in a home. And, in a perfect world, the little girl shouldn't be there either. Her mother, the Caregiver, should be able to afford child-care when the snow falls and the school closes. But there they are, Mr D forgetting the world around him while remembering a day no one else will ever remember – and the little girl, too impatient to stay hidden in a store-room on a snow day, but creeping out like Alice to meet these strange unearthly creatures who don't know who they are.

Around this encounter we meet the man's wife, Mrs D, trying to go on loving a man who thinks he has never met her; we meet the Clinician, who lost his mother to the disease, and who burns the midnight oil to find the 'thought that will light the sky'; and we meet the Caregiver, who dreams of a bright morning when she and the Clinician will go dancing through the corridors of the care home crying *eureka*! because the cure is found.

The care home in *The Lion's Face* is more run-down, more overstretched than some of the impressive places we visited – but it's better than some others we saw. The Clinician may be a little on the gauche side, the Caregiver's briskness may tilt to the insensitive (nor is hiding her daughter in the store-room a deed that might be called 'best practice'), while Mrs D can seem cruel at the end of her tether, but I wanted to show a human, credible situation, where real people try to cope as best they can with real misfortune and misery. And, as the story will tell, sometimes a child can heal what no one else can – even if it's a child who has no right to be there.

Glyn Maxwell

Coming Out of the Dark – Our Changing Relationship with Alzheimer's Disease

For much of the last century Alzheimer's disease was hidden, surfacing only in textbooks, known only to a few. First described in 1906 by Alois Alzheimer, for the first sixty or so years of its life, Alzheimer's disease was thought to be a rare disorder suffered by a small number of younger people – like its first reported victim, Auguste D., a woman in her early 50's. Why was this? Was it, as has been suggested, simply that older people were expected to be forgetful, in need of help, senile? Or was it that less was expected of older people, living with their families, passively respected as elders, largely ignored? Or was it perhaps that there were just fewer older people then? Whatever the reason, so much has changed in the last two or three decades. First were the careful, painstaking studies that showed that older people with dementia – memory failure together with an increasing inability to look after oneself – had the same changes in their brain as did Auguste D. Then came the epidemiologists, carefully graphing the rise in dementia in the elderly and the psychologists, showing that in the absence of this dementia, memory in the elderly does not fail, or at least not much. Finally in their wake came the laboratory scientists showing the molecular events that slowly yet relentlessly spread across the brain in Alzheimer's disease, leaving a wake of dying brain cells behind them.

Today, Alzheimer's disease is no longer an unspoken disease; quite the opposite in fact. Alzheimer's disease seems to have a regular slot in our newspapers, on the radio, on TV. The charities – the Alzheimer's Society and the Alzheimer's Research Trust – must take much of the credit for this, as they have done so much to raise the profile of the illness. This can only be a good thing: money is raised for research, politicians are compelled to fund better services, families no longer suffer alone. This news-related profile is built around two narratives – one of fear and one of hope. The fearful narrative tells the story of the 800,000 people with dementia in the UK, the £18 billion spent on caring for them and the rising tide of dementia patients and costs that come with an ageing population. Sometimes, too, we hear the story of those in the less developed world where the majority of people with dementia live and where in the absence of social care, with limited health services and with an increasingly urbanised population losing traditional family structures, those with dementia can be in a perilous situation. This fearful story is counterbalanced by the hopeful story of science and the search for therapy. This narrative is of untangling the molecular events in the brain, of finding the environmental and genetic influences of disease and of trials of new therapies.

Both narratives are true. It is true that Alzheimer's disease is common and costly and set to become more so. A million people with dementia by 2025; costs to the NHS, social services and families that outweigh the costs of heart disease and cancer combined. It is true, too, that the research is moving forward: we understand more about this disease than perhaps any other disorder of the brain and more than ten drugs are in late stage clinical trials with more than 50 following close behind. No-one knows if these multi-million pound experiments will result in a new treatment but it isn't unreasonable to hope that in ten years time we might see treatments in the clinic designed to slow the progression of the disorder.

However, both narratives also fail to tell the whole story. Missing from the news-related profile of Alzheimer's disease are the people touched by the illness. The patients, their families and carers, the diverse professionals are all shadowy figures, if they appear at all. Here in *The Lion's Face*, they take centre stage; they are the story. In this work, we see the narrative of fear (see for example the young daughter of the nurse) and that of hope (the scientists and the nurse), but it is the person with Alzheimer's disease that occupies our attention. The poetry and urgency of his words are as compelling and moving as those of every other character. It was for this reason that we wanted to work with The Opera Group. By spending time with the composer, Elena Langer, the librettist Glyn Maxwell, with the director John Fulljames and others we hoped to show them this story. The Opera Group team have immersed themselves in our world – have spent time in our laboratories and with our students and scientists, have sat with our multi-disciplinary teams of nurses, psychologists, occupational therapists and others, have talked with people with dementia and their family members. From this has emerged a story that we recognise – it is that of our patients and colleagues. We see some striking representations of dementia, some of which are so true that they might be used as teaching aids. But most of all we see refracted back to us in poetry, music and drama the story of the people touched by this disease. It is this story that should be told, and sung and acted.

Simon Lovestone
Felicity Callard
King's College London, Institute of Psychiatry
NIHR Biomedical Research Centre at the South London and Maudsley NHS
Foundation Trust

The Institute of Psychiatry at King's College London is a world-leading research organisation with a strong commitment to education and public engagement in science. Pioneering dementia researcher Professor Simon Lovestone enlisted colleagues from the MRC Centre for Neurodegeneration Research, South London and Maudsley NHS Foundation Trust (SLaM) and the NIHR BRC for Mental Health, to collaborate on this project. The MRC Centre has over 100 researchers involved in pre-clinical and early clinical research; the BRC is a new centre for biomedical research focussed on delivering new insights in technologies, techniques and treatments; and SLaM is the largest provider of mental health care in the UK treating more than 1,000 patients with dementia every year.

www.iop.kcl.ac.uk

The Lion's Face – The Meaning of the Title

John Bayley, in his widely read book *Iris: A Memoir of Iris Murdoch* (1998), writes that: 'The Alzheimer face has been clinically described as the "lion face". ... The features settle into a leonine impassivity which does remind one of the King of Beasts. ... The Alzheimer face indicates only an absence: it is a mask in the most literal sense'.

But, Bayley's conviction to the contrary, the history of medicine and of disability shows us that 'leonine impassivity' has been and continues to be more commonly clinically associated with facial descriptions of diseases other than Alzheimer's, particularly leprosy (*leonine facies*) and Parkinson's disease (*mask-like facies*). Indeed, the association between leprosy and a lion-like face dates at least as far back as medieval Arabic medicine. The connotations associated with leonine impassivity are, nonetheless, undoubtedly broad and resonant – and appear to be attached to conditions (such as Alzheimer's disease and leprosy) that commonly provoke fear and a sense of distance in the observer.

We might do well, then, to consider the words of the historian of disability M Miles, with whom I discussed the curious medical history of a lion-like face when helping The Opera Group to track the origins of this phrase. Miles suggests that: 'A number of things can happen to the face muscles, which may or may not reflect the emotional/psychological state of the face owner – it is mostly the observer who fits the tag, makes the picture of a lion (or an old goat, old dog, old trout, old hen, to name a few more creatures with whom we sometimes compare one another)'.

Felicity Callard, PhD
Historian and sociologist of psychiatry
Biomedical Research Centre for Mental Health, South London & Maudsley
NHS Foundation Trust and Institute of Psychiatry, King's College London

What is Dementia?

The word dementia is an umbrella term which describes a serious deterioration in mental functions, such as memory, language, orientation and judgment.

A common question asked is whether Alzheimer's disease and dementia are the same thing. The answer is both yes and no. Alzheimer's disease is one cause of dementia, but several other diseases can cause it too. Alzheimer's disease is the most common cause of dementia, accounting for two thirds of cases in the elderly. Other diseases that cause dementia are vascular dementia which includes multi-infarct dementia and Binswanger's disease, dementia with Lewy Bodies, and fronto-temporal dementia. It is not uncommon for people to have more than one form of dementia; for example, some people with vascular dementia also have Alzheimer's.

The symptoms of Alzheimer's are caused by nerve cells dying in certain areas of the brain and the deterioration of millions of connections between affected nerve cells. The loss of connections in the part of the brain dealing with memory usually causes the first symptoms. The disease progresses and spreads, gradually affecting cells in other parts of the brain.

More research is needed to find out what causes the nerve cells to die. Different types of protein deposits, known as amyloid plaques and tau tangles, accumulate in the brains of Alzheimer's patients, but it is not yet known whether these actually cause the disease or are a symptom of it. Research targeting these two proteins is ongoing, with scientists understanding more every day about how and why they accumulate, how to clear the deposits and how to prevent them forming in the first place.

The Alzheimer's Research Trust's aim is simple - we want to combat dementia once and for all. We fund world-class scientific research to find ways to prevent, cure or treat Alzheimer's disease and related dementias, including vascular dementia, dementia with Lewy Bodies and fronto-temporal dementia.

As the number of people with dementia rises, there is an urgent need to develop new treatments. The Alzheimer's Research Trust funds research across the UK and beyond. We consult with scientists on the best way to support research and fund innovative work by the most promising researchers to take us towards new treatments.

Each year the charity commits to more grants, and with over 140 projects supported across the UK right now, our understanding of dementia and how to defeat it becomes more complete every day.

To find out more about dementia and our mission to defeat it, visit our website at www.alzheimers-research.org.uk or call 01223 843899

Alzheimer's Society | Leading the fight against dementia

Alzheimer's Society is the UK's leading support and research charity for people with dementia and those who care for them.

> "It's such a shock when you own husband doesn't know who you are any more. After being married for 62 years...well, it breaks your heart."
> *Ruby, whose husband Denis has the Alzheimer's disease*

Dementia: the picture today:

- 750,000 people with dementia in the UK, with numbers set to rise to one million by 2025.
- One in 3 people over 65 will die with dementia.
- Currently, dementia costs the UK £20 billion a year

Alzheimer's Society supports people to live well with dementia today and funds research to find a cure tomorrow. We rely on voluntary donations to continue our vital work:

- Alzheimer's Society campaigns for and champions the rights of people living with dementia and the millions of people who care for them.
- Alzheimer's Society provides information and support for people with all forms of dementia and those who care for them through its publications, dementia help lines and local services
- We fund an innovative programme of biomedical and social research in the areas of cause, cure and care.

To make a donation to Alzheimer's Society please call: 0845 306 0898 and quote "Community Fundraising" OR for more information about our services across the country and those close to you, please visit www.alzheimers.org.uk or call 020 7423 3500

Registered charity No.296645

the Opera group

The Opera Group tours opera and music theatre across the UK and internationally – re-creating rarely performed gems and commissioning fresh new works from the artists of the future. One thing defines everything we do: an unshakeable belief in the power of telling stories by bringing together outstanding theatre and live music. We work in collaboration with a variety of partners who share our passion for reaching the widest possible audience.

The Opera Group is an Associate Company of the Young Vic and also collaborates regularly with ROH2 at the Royal Opera House. The Opera Group's work has been recognised with the Best Musical Award at the Evening Standard Theatre Awards 2008 for *Street Scene* as well as Best Stagework at the British Composer Awards 2004 for *Birds. Barks. Bones. The Enchanted Pig* was shortlisted for the Best Opera and Music Theatre Award at the 2006 Royal Philharmonic Society Awards and in 2009 *Into the Little Hill* was shortlisted for a Southbank Show Award.

Artistic Director	John Fulljames
Executive Producer	Sherry Neyhus
General Manager	Alison Porter
Assistant Producer	Allison Rosser
Press and PR	Faith Wilson Arts Publicity
Marketing	Ben Jefferies for makes three marketing + promotion
Development	Michelle Wright for Cause4
Education Associate	Nina Swann
Finance	Sandra Francis-Love
Trustees	Claudia Pendred (chair), David Bernstein, Lindsey Glen, John Gilhooly, Paul Kearney, Anthony Newhouse, Andrew Newman

The Opera Group
c/o Young Vic, 66 The Cut, London, SE1 8LZ
020 7922 2846
enquiries@theoperagroup.co.uk
theoperagroup.co.uk

The Opera Group is a company limited by guarantee registered in England No. 3508706
Registered Charity No. 1070013 VAT No. 749404416

PRSFoundation for new music   **The Eranda Foundation**

2006: *The Nose, Blond Eckbert*
2007: *The Enchanted Pig, The Shops*
2008: *Street Scene, Varjak Paw*
2009: *Into the Little Hill / Down by the Greenwood Side, The Enchanted Pig*
2010: *The Lion's Face, Recital I / Into the Little Hill, The Human Comedy*

Join Us

The Opera Group pioneers the development and presentation of brand new musical storytelling that merges the best of contemporary theatre and music. Over the last year The Opera Group has developed a new model of contemporary opera which integrates social and community partners into the full process of developing, producing and touring a new opera, allowing the company to enrich its work and engage new audiences in more meaningful ways. Our programme of work for 2011 and 2012 will exploit our strong network of co-producing relationships and will ensure a full programme of boldly new commissioned work as well as revivals of previous acclaimed work.

In order to bring these productions to life, The Opera Group relies on the support of a wide-ranging group of funders — individuals, sponsors, trusts and foundations. We invite you to join us as we continue to explore, develop and produce new ideas and develop the most exciting new productions.

Become an OperaGroupie!

The Opera Groupies are key supporters of The Opera Group. For as little as £100 a year anyone can become an OperaGroupie and gain an insight into the development of a new opera. Join now and you can enjoy the following benefits:
- Acknowledgement of your support in our programmes and on our website.
- Meet the cast and each other and see the difference your contribution makes at private model showings, exclusive presentations and open rehearsals.
- Purchase tickets to exclusive opening night performances and post-show parties.

The Opera Groupies: Sherban Canacuzino, Albert Edwards, John Fulljames, Ian Hamilton, David Howie, Robert and Lindsey Kaye, Thomas Lingard, Alison McNaught, Andrew Newman, Claudia Pendred, Ed Ross, Virginia Rushton, Christian Wells

How to join the Groupies: Call Sherry Neyhus on 020 7922 2846 or email producer@theoperagroup.co.uk

The Opera Group is grateful to the following for their support of our work in 2009-2010: The Apple Pickers Foundation, Anonymous, Arts Council England, Columbia Foundation, Geoffrey Collens, The D'Oyly Carte Foundation, Vernon and Hazel Ellis, The Eranda Foundation, Esmée Fairbairn Foundation, Golsoncott Foundation, The Harold Hyam Wingate Foundation, Into the Little Hill Syndicate, Jerwood Charitable Foundation, Jerwood Space, The Leche Trust, The Linbury Trust, The Lynn Foundation, The Mackintosh Foundation, Robert McFarland, Anthony Newhouse, N Smith Charitable Trust, The Peter Moores Foundation, Performing Rights Society Foundation, Wellcome Trust, David M Wells

Elena Langer *Composer*

Elena Langer is a Moscow-born and London-based composer. She graduated from the Tchaikovsky Moscow Conservatoire and from the Royal Academy of Music (PhD). Lena has written compositions in diverse genres, including opera and multimedia, orchestral, chamber and choral works and has received commissions and performances from international ensembles, festivals and organisations such as The Royal Opera House's ROH2, Zurich Opera (Switzerland), the Almeida Opera Festival (UK), The Britten and Strauss Festival in Aldeburgh (UK), Gaudeamus New Music Week (Netherlands), Moscow Autumn Festival (Russia), Warsaw Autumn Festival (Poland), Park Lane Group (UK), State of the Nation Festival (UK), Chamber Music Series "XX/XXI" of the Bayerische Staatsoper (Germany), Sounds Undeground (UK) and the Canterbury Festival (UK). Some of her works have been commercially recorded on the Black Box Label (UK), Quartz Music (UK), Usk (UK) and Universal Music Russia, and some broadcast on BBC Radio 3, BBC World Service, Radio Echo of Moscow and Dutch Radio.

Glyn Maxwell *Writer*

Glyn Maxwell has published several books of poetry, including *The Nerve*, which won the Geoffrey Faber Memorial Prize, and *Hide Now*, which was shortlisted for both the TS Eliot and Forward Prizes last year. In 1997 he was awarded the E.M.Forster Prize for his work by the American Academy of Arts and Letters. His plays have been staged in London, New York and Edinburgh, and include *The Lifeblood*, which was British Theatre Guide's 'Best Play' at the Edinburgh Fringe in 2004, *Broken Journey* and *The Only Girl in the World*, both Time Out Critics' Choices. His play *Mimi and the Stalker* is in development as a screenplay with an award from the UK Film Council. His opera work includes *Ariadne* and *The Girl of Sand*, both with Elena Langer for the Almeida Opera Festival, *The Birds*, with Ed Hughes and *I Fagiolini*, and, in 2011, *Seven Angels*, with Luke Bedford.

COMPANY BIOGRAPHIES

Dave Hill *Mr D*

Music has been an important thread running through Dave's career, from writing and singing for *The Ken Campbell Road Show* to *Corunna* with Steeleye Span (The Royal Court) and *The Mysteries* with the Albion Band and *Lark Rise to Candleford* with the Home Service (National Theatre). He has co-written two musicals – *Bendigo* and *Walking Like Geoffrey* (Nottingham Playhouse). He played God in Benjamin Britten's *Noah's Flood* (The Aldeburgh Festival).

His theatre credits include *Breaking the Code* (Haymarket), *The Crucible* (The National & Comedy Theatre). *Gloo Joo* (Criterion), *The Comedians* (Nottingham Playhouse and Wyndhams Theatre), Richard III, Antony & Cleopatra and Somson Agonistes (Northern Broadside) and *Trackers of Oxyrincus* (Delphi Theatre, Greece).

His film credits include Peter Greenaway's *Draughtsman's Contract*, *Prometheus*, *There's Only One Jimmy Grimble*, *Car Trouble*, *Remembrance* and *The Full Monty*. His many television credits include *Chef*, *City Central*, *Linda Green*, *Bob & Rose*, *Place of Execution*, *Rocket Man*, *Take A Girl Like You*, *New Tricks*, *Caravaggio*, *Real Women*, *The Ice House*, *Cracker*, *Midsomer Murders*, *Wallander* and *EastEnders*.

Elizabeth Sikora *Mrs D*

Born in Scotland, Elizabeth studied at the Royal Scottish Academy of Music and Drama and in London. Her credits include, for the Royal Opera House, Filipyevna in *Eugene Onegin*, Third Lady in *Die Zauberflöte*, Giovanna in *Rigoletto*, Annina in *La traviata*, Rossweisse in *Die Walküre* and Maddalena in *Linda di Chamounix* (Royal Opera in concert) She has sung in *Les Noces* and *Mayerling* (Royal Ballet), *Mahler's Five Rückert Lieder* at the Royal Festival Hall (English National Ballet). She has appeared in *Khovanshchina* (English National Opera), *Death of Klinghoffer* (Scottish Opera), *Les Contes d'Hoffmann* (Nationiale Reisopera), *Cunning Little Vixen* and *Peter Grimes* (Geneva Opera), Marcellina in *Le nozze di Figaro* (Festival Rotas dos Monumentos in Portugal). *Andrea Chenier* and *Cendrillon* (Chelsea Opera Group), *Margot la Rouge* (BBC SO), *A Streetcar Named Desire* (LSO), Gertrude in *Roméo et Juliette* (Concertgebouw) and Prole Woman in *1984* (La Scala).

Rachel Hynes *Caregiver*

Rachel trained at the Royal Scottish Academy of Music and Drama and continues her studies with Patricia Hay and Llyndall Trotman. Her credits include Ellen Orford in *Peter Grimes* (Opera North), Freia in *Das Rheingold*, Helmwige in *Die Walküre*, Third Norn in *Götterdämmerung*, Euridice in *Orfeo ed Euridice*, First Lady in *The Magic Flute*, Mimi in *La Boheme*, The Dew Fairy in *Hansel & Gretel* and Giannetta in *L'Elisir d'Amore* (all Scottish Opera), Denise in *The Knot Garden* (Montepulciano, Scottish Opera, BBC Symphony Orchestra), 4th Maid in *Elektra* (Edinburgh Festival), Cara in David Bruce's *Push!* (Tête à Tête). Rachel is a regular soloist at the Llanelli Proms.

Fflur Wyn *Caregiver's Daughter*
Fflur recently graduated from the Royal Academy of Music Opera Course. In 2005 she won first prize and the audience prize at the National Handel Competition in London. Her credits include Sophie in *Werther* (Opera North), Haydn in *Harmoniemesse* (Northern Sinfonia), Barbarina in *Le Nozze di Figaro* (La Monnaie, Brussels), Haydn *Creation* (London Mozart Players), Handel *Messiah* (English Concert), Iphis in *Jephtha* (Welsh National Opera), Papagena and cover Pamina in *The Magic Flute*, Clorida in *Kaiser's Croesus*, Gretel in *Hansel and Gretel*, Giulietta *Capuleti in e I Montecchi* (Opera North) Pamina (Holland Park Opera), Barbarina in *Le Nozze di Figaro* (Garsington Opera), Karolka in Janá ek *Jenufa* (St Endellion Music Festival).

Benedict Nelson

Clinician-Scientist
Benedict studied at the Guildhall school of Music and Drama and the National Opera Studio. In 2007 Benedict won second prize in the Kathleen Ferrier awards and the Guildhall Gold Medal. His credits include Aeneas in *Dido and Aeneas*, Count Almaviva, Figaro in *Le Nozze di Figaro*, Masetto, Don Giovanni in *Don Giovanni*, Sprecher in *Die Zauberflote*, Marcello in *La Boheme*, Demetrius in *A Midsummer Night's Dream*, Sid in *Albert Herring*, Don Parmenione in *L'occasione fa il ladro*, Christian in *Un ballo in maschera*, Zurga in *Les pêcheurs de perles*, Morales in *Carmen*, Tarquinius and Junius in *Rape of Lucretia*. Future engagements include debuts with the CBSO and Andris Nelsons, the RPO, Nantes Opera and English National Opera.

Harry Bradford *Boy*

Born in London, Harry attends the City of London School holding both academic and music scholarships. A member of the Chapel Royal Choir, he first appeared with them at the Princess Diana Memorial Concert. Following the release of his debut album, Harry passed both the Dip. LCM and Dip.ABRSM (classical singing) with distinction. Winner of BBC Radio 2's Young Chorister of the Year 2008/9, Harry has performed on BBC 1's "Songs of Praise" and many radio broadcasts. His credits include *The Magic Flute* and *Messiah* (English National Opera) as well as *The Cunning Little Vixen* (Royal Opera House). Concert performances include The Royal Festival Hall, Selwyn College, Cambridge and Belgium with Fanfareorkest Brass-aux-Saxes.

Jonathan Bircumshaw *Boy*

Jonathan joined the New London Children's Choir in 2009 and shortly afterwards began studying voice with Jenny Lilleystone. In the spring he took part in the ENO production of *Peter Grimes* and in the summer sang in the chorus for *Hansel and Gretel* (Opera Holland Park). He attends the Rudolf Steiner School in Kings Langley. His many enthusiasms include fishing, mountaineering, kayaking, sailing, snowboarding and cycling.

CREATIVE TEAM

Nicholas Collon *Conductor*

As Principal Conductor of Aurora Orchestra, British conductor Nicholas studied at Clare College, Cambridge and is establishing an enviable reputation as an inspirational interpreter in an exceptionally wide range of music. Aurora has performed at the Aldeburgh and the Barbican Young Genius Festivals, the BBC Proms and at LSO St Luke's to great acclaim. Other recent work includes concerts with Opera North, the London Sinfonietta and Symphonieorchester Vorarlberg (Austria).

His recent operatic work includes Walton's *The Bear* and Stravinsky's *Renard* (Mahogany Opera). In 2007 he conducted Mozart's *The Magic Flute*, directed by Sam West, in Ramallah and Bethlehem, and returned last year with performances of *La Boheme*.

This season his engagements include a week's curatorship at King's Place featuring music from the Weimar Republic and work with the Britten Sinfonia. Future appearances with Aurora Orchestra include concerts at LSO St Luke's, Aldeburgh Festival, the London Sinfonietta, Wigmore Hall, BBC Proms and King's Place.

John Fulljames *Director*

John is Artistic Director of The Opera Group for whom his productions include *Into the Little Hill*, *Street Scene*, Judith Weir's *Blond Eckbert*, Shostakovich's *The Nose* and the world premieres of Julian Phillips's *Varjak Paw*, Edward Rushton's *The Shops,* Ed Hughes's *The Birds* and the original and revival productions of *The Enchanted Pig*. Other recent productions include *The Excursions of Mr Broucek*, *Roméo et Juliette*, *Saul* and *Hansel and Gretel* (Opera North), *Gianni Schicchi*, *Florentine Tragedy* and *Mavra* (Greek National Opera), *Snegurochka* and *Susannah* (Wexford Festival, winner, Irish Theatre Awards Best Opera), *Tobias and the Angel* (Young Vic and English Touring Opera) and *Nabucco* (Opera Holland Park).

Alex Lowde *Designer*

For The Opera Group: *The Nose*, *Candide*, and *The Threepenny Opera*. Alex trained at Hull University and Motley Theatre Design Course. In 2007 Alex was part of the UK team exhibiting at the Prague Quadrennial, with his designs for *Tobias and the Angel*. Current and recent work includes *The Adventures of Mr Broucek* (Opera North and Scottish Opera), *The Elephant Man* and *Equus* (Dundee Rep). Previous work includes *Beauty and The Beast* (Dundee Rep), *Beyond the Rave* (a film for download on Myspace and DVD Pure Grass Films), *Le Nozze di Figaro* (Sadler's Wells and Buxton Festival), *Paradise Moscow* (Royal Academy of Music), *The Gentle Giant* (Royal Opera House Education, Linbury Theatre and tour), *Tobias and the Angel* (Young Vic and English Touring Opera), *Triptych* (Cambridge University), *Angelic to Alnwick* and *Romeo & Juliet* (Newcastle Playhouse), new writing season for Paines Plough (Finborough Theatre).

Jon Clark *Lighting Designer*
For The Opera Group: *Into The Little Hill/Down by the Greenwood Side, Street Scene*. Jon's theatre credits include *The Cat in the Hat, Pains of Youth, Our Class, Women of Troy* (National Theatre), *King Lear, The Winter's Tale, The Merchant of Venice* (Royal Shakespeare Company), *Polar Bears* (Donmar Warehouse), *The Little Dog Laughed* (Garrick), *Three Days of Rain* (Apollo), *The Lover & The Collection, Dickens Unplugged* (Comedy), *Pinter's People* (Haymarket), *Aunt Dan & Lemon, The Pride, Gone Too Far!* (Royal Court), *Been So Long, The Jewish Wife, How Much Is Your Iron?* (Young Vic). His opera credits include *The Love for Three Oranges* (Scottish Opera & Royal Scottish Academy of Music and Drama), *Jenufa* (revival for English National Opera, Washington Opera), *I Capuleti e I Montecchi, L'Elisir d'Amore, The Barber of Seville, Cosi Fan Tutte* (Grange Park Opera). Dance credits include Cathy Marston's *Clara, Libera Me,* Karole Armitage's *Between The Clock and The Bed,* A new piece for Andrea Miller (Bern Ballett), *Tenderhook, Sorry for the Missiles* (Scottish Dance Theatre).

Ian William Galloway
Projection Designer
Ian is a video designer and director working with film and live visuals in performance. His credits include *The Kreuzter Sonata, Nocturnal* (Gate Theatre), *Medea/Medea* (Headlong), *The Spanish Tragedy* (Arcola), *Proper Clever* (Liverpool Playhouse), *The Tempest* (Lightworks & Parrabolla),

Blood (Royal Court), *Starvin* (Fitzgerald & Stapleton), *Julius Caesar* (Barbican), *A Minute Too Late, Battleship Potemkin* (Complicite), *Hitchcock Blonde* (Alley Theatre Houston & South Coast Repertory LA) and *Hotel de Pekin* (Nationale Reisopera Holland), as well as designing for live music and directing various shorts and promos. He works as part of Mesmer, a collaboration of video and projection designers working in theatre, dance, opera, fashion and music.

Fergus O'Hare *Sound Designer*
For The Opera Group: *Street Scene*. Fergus' recent credits includes *Peter and Vandy* (503), Sebastian Faulk's *Birdsong* (Workshop), *Inherit The Wind* (Old Vic), *The Black Album* (National Theatre), *Much Ado About Nothing, Tempest, Importance of Being Earnest* (Regent's Park), *Julius Caesar* (Royal Shakespeare Company), *Pictures From An Exhibition, In The Red and Brown Water* (Young Vic), *Alphabetical Order* (Hampstead Theatre), *Twelfth Night* (Donmar West End), *Cordelia Dream* (Royal Shakespeare Company), *Marble* (Abbey Theatre). Work in New York, Los Angeles and Sydney includes *The Shape of Things, A Day in the Death of Joe Egg, Dance of Death, Noises Off, Electra* (Drama Desk Nominee) and *An Enemy of the People*.

Lucy Bradley *Assistant Director*
Lucy studied drama at Middlesex University and has worked as a theatre practitioner and director for the past 5 years. Her directing credits include *An Ode to My Sisters* (Images of Elsewhere), *Aladdin*,

Cinderella and *Lord of the Flies* (all for West Wing, Slough), *Shuti and Together* (lala at Theatre 503 and The Arcola) and *Not loving Susan* (Kings Head Theatre). Assistant Directing credits include *Street Scene* (The Opera Group, Young Vic and Watford Palace Theatre), *Knight Crew* (Glyndebourne), *The Wedding: or the rime of the Ancient Mariner* (Young Vic and South Bank Centre), *The Deranged Marriage* (Rifco Arts). Lucy is the Creative Director of Peckham Shed an inclusive youth theatre company in South East London.

Sherry Neyhus
Executive Producer
Sherry joined The Opera Group as the company's first Executive Producer in 2006 producing the UK tour of the original production of *The Enchanted Pig* and its recent 2009 revival (which also visited the New Victory Theater in New York), the world premieres of *The Shops* and *Varjak Paw* and the revivals of *Street Scene* and *Into the Little Hill*. Sherry has worked in arts management for 20 years joining the acclaimed Bathhouse Theatre in Seattle in 1989. An experienced fund developer and events manager, she was responsible for two of Seattle's major cultural events – the Seattle Art Museum's Black and White Ball (1996) and the grand re-opening of the Henry Art Gallery (1997). Since re-locating to London in 1998 to earn an M.A. at Goldsmith's College, she has worked at the Theatre Royal Stratford East and the National Theatre before joining The Opera Group.

THE LION'S FACE

Glyn Maxwell

THE LION'S FACE

Music by Elena Langer

OBERON BOOKS
LONDON

Libretto first published by Oberon Books Ltd in 2010
521 Caledonian Road, London N7 9RH
Tel: 020 7607 3637 / Fax: 020 7607 3629
e-mail: info@oberonbooks.com
www.oberonbooks.com

The Lion's Face

Micheline Steinberg Associates
104 Great Portland Street
London W1W 6PE

The vocal or full score and orchestral parts are available from Elena Langer (www.elenalanger.com) directly or through The Opera Group.

A catalogue record for this book is available from the British Library.

Cover design by Module Media

ISBN: 978-1-84002-994-9

Printed in Great Britain by CPI Antony Rowe, Chippenham.

ACT ONE

A Boy is looking in a window. He sees reflected in it the face of an Old Man.

An Old Man is looking in a window. This is MR D, *in a chair, in his care home.*

VOICES OF BOYS
At the end of the day
when it's time and it's time to
you will want to go home
you will be home anyway
you will want to go home anyway
when it's time and it's time to
at the end of the day
when it's time to

MR D
the doctor was my doctor
the doctor was
there was the different doctor
the different doctor there
the different
he had the best results
he had the best results
he had the best
they never come the same
people never come here
people come here
two ladies held the picture
of the boy beside the seaside
to be beside
to be beside I
buy him the ice-cream!
buy him the ice-cream
beside the side I
said I have the things
I have the things
there's money in the land
to buy the things but no
beside they say no
they fold the boy away
in the white ice-cream book
in the white book
the different doctor closing
time in the white book

the doctor is my doctor
where is my white doctor
who comes who came before
no one ever
comes who came before

MRS D is visiting. Outside, snow is falling.

MRS D
It started in the night
and now it's everywhere
it doesn't look like stopping
and only yesterday
there were nine daffodils
the crocuses had come
I counted them for you
there were nine daffodils

The boys will be here soon
your sons
as soon as soon can be

A sunny autumn Saturday
seventy months ago
he brings them laughing to his own front door
they bring him laughing to his own front door
the tears roll down his face
the tears roll down his face
he says he must have gone some way
he didn't know
he knows he must have gone some way
he didn't know
the way
he didn't know

A windy day, a Wednesday
it must have been
he brought policemen back from town with him
policemen brought him back from town with them
the tears roll down his face
the tears roll down his face

they found him on a roundabout
he didn't know
he lay down on a roundabout
he didn't know
the time
he didn't know

> *Husband and wife alone, and the snow falling still. They open a photograph album.*

MR D	MRS D
I rolled out on a lane of bells	It started in the night
a lane of bells towards a town	and now it's everywhere
of bells I need to keep this secret	
I remember thinking	
I rolled out on a lane of bells	it doesn't look like stopping
I lay down in a road of grass	and only yesterday
not a road where engines come to	there were nine daffodils
rivers with no waters in them	the crocuses had come
me in place of water	I counted them for you
I lay down in a road of grass	there were nine daffodils
I rolled out on a	
merrily merrily well I knew	
I was not water I remember	
water raging at me	
red, red buses	
circle all about	
big top of circle elephants	the boys will be here soon
and I was master of the rainstorm	
I remember thinking	
rain master I remember thinking	your sons your sons
not a road and round and round me	as soon as soon can be
number six and number sixty	the boys will be here soon
number five and number fifty	your sons
I remember thinking number	as soon as soon can be
forty number forty-*A*	
the boys will be here soon	
I don't know how I came home	
how I came home from the circle how?	

29

the boys will be here soon
how I
came home

VOICES OF BOYS
at the end of the day
and it's time and is time to
will want to go home
when it's time to

MRS D departs, leaving MR D with the photograph album, at which he looks blankly.

As he does we see, on the screen, faint black-and-white photos of children – a class photograph from the 1930s. Suddenly the children start moving, singing. Then we start to see things...

Glimpses of a 1930s fair – a merry-go-round with nobody on it, empty swings still swinging. Then a big house set in a garden. Then we seem to be running through the garden, chasing someone who runs too fast and is only glimpsed for a second – the bouncing long hair of a girl – but she disappears ahead and the picture fades to snow.

Elsewhere in the Home, a Girl, THE CAREGIVER's DAUGHTER, is hiding in a store-room. She looks out of the window at the snow.

THE DAUGHTER
I woke up
like every day
the world was all
blue and snow
was falling
snow just like
Christmas morning
snow but I never
seen snow
at Christmas I never
seen snow at all but snow
was all I saw
the falling
snow the settling

snow the shining
snow, no one has to
go to school now
snow has fallen
snow has buried
school and everywhere
snow men
make snow men

THE CAREGIVER has come to give MR D a meal.

MR D
we had green tickets in a roll
and every roll was full of tickets
we had green tickets
all the rides you needed tickets

THE CAREGIVER
Pineapple pineapple, look,
you liked it when you tried it
mango, no
you like it, like it

we had green tickets
all the rides you needed tickets
the rides

MRS D arrives again.

MRS D
The rides again
some fair there never was for me
and won't be ever

THE CAREGIVER
Melon green
and melon orange

MR D
the fair has come
it isn't always there!

MRS D
It isn't always there

THE CAREGIVER
Melon green
and melon orange, look
you liked it when you tried it
mango, no
you like it, like it, like it!

MR D
it comes on Fridays
I shall collect her on the way

MRS D
It comes on rainy days
some fair there never was for me
and won't be ever
never was for me
rides
again

THE CAREGIVER
Melon green and melon orange
melon green and melon orange
of course

MR D
I shall collect her on the way

of course you shall, let's cut this up

I shall collect her
O she has to hold my hand
or I shall scream!

of course you shall, it comes and goes

or I shall scream!

of course you shall and open wide
open wide open wide

MRS D
Or *I* shall scream
I shall scream

THE CAREGIVER
Now open wide here comes the special
breakfast ride and down we go

MR D
we had green tickets in a roll
I shall collect her
the fair has come
she has to hold my hand
I shall collect her!

MRS D
A fair there never was for me
he held a hand that isn't there

THE CAREGIVER
Of course you shall collect her
of course she'll hold your hand

MRS D
Of course she will
of course she will
she'll hold your hand
she'll wave you off

32

The breakfast is finished. MRS D departs, and so does THE CAREGIVER.

THE DAUGHTER grows impatient in the store-room.

THE DAUGHTER
I have to wait for mum in here
I'm all alone
I'm not supposed to make a sound
or they might come
I'm killing time imagining
I'm one of them
I'm killing time imagining
I'm one of them
one of them
one of them –
oh my god imagine
oh my god imagine
oh my god
oh!
No
they'll have cured it when I'm ancient
that's well known
no they'll have cured it when I'm ancient
that's well known
well known

THE CLINICIAN-SCIENTIST comes to visit MR D.

MR D
somebody comes and no one's told him
somebody comes and no one's
no one's told him

THE CLINICIAN-SCIENTIST
And how are we, my friend?

pleased to meet you always a pleasure
sit yourself down
always a pleasure

Look at that snow
look at that snow
warm and cosy
warm and cosy

sit yourself down

Shall we look at our questions?

ask me the questions
I will help you doctor
ask me the questions

What is the year?

the new year

What is the day?

today

What is the season?

snowtime

Where are we?

hometime

What is this country?

england

What is this town?

england

What am I holding? *[It's an apple]*

questions

What am I holding? *[It's a pencil]*

it's warm and cosy

Take your time

no one's told him
it's warm and cosy
you have a pencil
you have a
apple
you have a peach
you have a petal
a piece of paper!   Can you read what it says?
                                      Can you do what it tells you?

I can read what it says   Can you do what it tells you?
I can read what it says   Can you do what it tells you?
I have finished with this

here it is
it's a paper
it answers the questions
what is the season
snow
is the season
always a pleasure
close your eyes
close your eyes

over the garden I am walking to see her

                What's that, my friend?

that's how I come
on a pink rose pathway I look at my present

                It's somebody's birthday?

I stop for a time
it is cloudy outside as I wrap my present

                You've bought her a present?

where is my present? It is given already
I gave her the present

                You gave her the present

she's running away, we had better catch her!

                Is this hide and seek?

it's my turn now

the whole of the garden
not in the greenhouse

                Not in the greenhouse?

we went to the fair, we had green tickets

                To go on the rides

we had green tickets
close your eyes
close your eyes

always a pleasure
I am pleased to meet you

doctor england
doctor england

look at the snow time!

> *MR D gazes blankly out of the window. THE CLINICIAN-SCIENTIST scribbles*
> *some notes in his book, then takes his leave, passing by THE CAREGIVER,*
> *who watches him with admiration.*

THE CAREGIVER
They say he's close to breaking through
then I can say I knew him!
you wouldn't think he's anyone
he looks the same as me and you
they say he's close to breaking through
then I can say I knew him!

His mother passed away with it
he doesn't know I know that
he always has a laugh with me
they say he's working day and night
his mother passed away from it
he doesn't know I know that
he always has a laugh with me

O I believe in him!
one day he'll shout *eureka*!
he'll run through all the corridors
he'll pick me up and dance with me
I'll be the first to know
the day we dance and sing *eureka!*

> *THE CAREGIVER continues on her rounds.*

VOICES OF BOYS
At the end of the day
when it's time and it's time to
you will want to go home

you will be home anyway
you will be home

MR D's eyes are closed. On the screen we see snow, and then a still image: the deserted merry-go-round. Then it starts turning, we see the empty swings still going, then the garden again, the door of the big house. We see a birthday cake, boys running, then a grand circular staircase, a girl descending it, her face hidden by a hat. The garden again, under darker sky: the girl darting ahead of us, going behind a tree – a glimpse to the right, to the left – we rush round the tree and there's no one. Then a wrapped present in a girl's hands, tearing it open – the present thrown away – pouring rain – the present abandoned in the mud...

MR D wakes distraught. The screen goes blank. He calls out, no one comes.

THE CAREGIVER, who should be attending to him, has had to go back to the store-room, where her DAUGHTER is restlessly waiting.

THE DAUGHTER	THE CAREGIVER
I know you'll say no	No
I know you'll say no	No
I want to go outside now	
and make a snowman	
make a snowman	No
it's not fair being stuck in here	Nobody knows you're here
it's not fair	I'll lose my job if they find you!
	I'll lose my job if they find you
it's not fair	and then we'll starve
being stuck in here	and then we'll starve
snowball fight!	you can't
snowball fight!	you can't
snowball fight	
snowball fight	the answer is no no no no no no
you can't say no to me	
I don't know who you are	a silly game and I've no time
I've never seen you before!	a silly game
don't touch me!	

don't touch me!
are you the cleaning lady?   a silly game and I've no time
I don't know who you are   a silly game
you like *them* more than me   what a silly thing to say
you talk to them all day
and they don't know who you are!
they don't know who *they* are!
every time they see you
is the first time they've ever!
you like them more than me

                                                   they need more looking after

I need more looking after!

                                                   they need more looking after

I – I don't need looking after!
I don't know who you are   I'll take you home
                                                              take you home soon
every time I see you   soon I'll take you home
is the first time I've ever!   I'll take you home

I don't know where my home is   not a nice thing to say
I don't know where my home is   not a nice thing to say
I don't know   not nice

I've forgotten what I said!
nothing's nice or not-nice
if I don't know what I said

I've forgotten what I said!
I've forgotten what I said!
I've forgotten –
play with your old snow men!

    THE CAREGIVER flees the store-room. She returns to MR D.

                                                              THE CAREGIVER
                                                          morning again my friend

MR D
I answer all the questions

                                                          morning again my friend

I am helping the white doctor

                    a stranger every single morning
                    like I just appear from nothing

I answer all   a stranger
I answer all the questions
I am helping the white doctor   I know you are
                         I know you are

have *you* got any questions?

               is it going to snow all day?

have *you* got any questions?

               is it going to snow all day?

I have got some questions
I have got some questions   you can ask me anything
                   you can ask me anything
                         ask me, ask

MR D trails off and goes quiet. THE CAREGIVER leaves.

MR D
why have you gone away?
you always go away
who are you?
come back
who
who are you
I
I have got some questions mrs
white I mrs
mrs white I
miss u!
w
mrs w
mrs u
mrs u?
mrs u!

*Suddenly he finds something hysterically funny and laughs uncontrollably
until the thought fades.*

Alone, THE CLINICIAN-SCIENTIST is looking at his notes. Then he closes the book and gazes into space.

THE CLINICIAN-SCIENTIST
Mum do you remember
do you remember forgetting your own son?
do you remember?
shape in a mist
a scientist
works on and on and on

Mum it's me grown up
a man in a white coat
filing away
at the end of the day
what he learned from it

trying to think the thought
that will light the sky!
but the night goes by
no sign of it

MRS D arrives at the Care Home. THE CLINICIAN-SCIENTIST has a consent form he wants her to sign.

MRS D
Today it isn't him at all
so why should it be me?
why can't I be a passer-by
a shadow strolling
somebody else's wife?
making in somebody's life
some memory O
leaving in somebody's life
a trace of me

THE CLINICIAN-SCIENTIST
I'd like to try and help him

Oh I'd like that too

this memory that troubles him
if we could find the key to it

> what could we do?

if we could find the key to it

> what happens then?
> the birthday and the fairground ride
> somebody who's more to him
> than all the world
> what happens then?

we understand
we learn from him

> what do you want from me?

we want to know
what we don't know
we want to see
where we can't see
we want to know
we want to see

> you want to save
> what you can't save
> I'm sorry
> I'm not myself

MRS D signs the consent form.

THE CLINICIAN-SCIENTIST   **MRS D**
Dear lady   Here is the name
                                                        of somebody
believe me   I used to be
believe me   forgive me
believe me   forgive me

MRS D leaves. THE CLINICIAN-SCIENTIST goes.

MR D catches sight of himself in the window.

MR D
excuse me
excuse me in the world

excuse me in the whole
in the hole in the hall
excuse me in the hall
is an old man in the hall
is an old man who looks
is an old man in the square
in the square in the open square
the winter in the square the
the window in the window

> *THE DAUGHTER has sneaked out of the store-room, and has wandered into the room. She watches MR D, unnoticed. She is fascinated.*

MR D
excuse me and he looks
he looks out of the window
an old man looking at me now
I don't know who that is
can you not say who that is?
he is asking who I am
who I am?
tell him who I am
tell him I am in my rights
he looks furious at me
he looks he doesn't know
what I'm doing here he does not seem to
want a schoolboy here!
tell him who I am for I am in my rights
tell him I am in my rights
he is breathing in breathing out
he is kinder than he was
he is kinder than the ladies
and all the different doctors
he is kinder it's all right
he is nodding I am in my rights
I will walk away look look
he is walking away too
he is sorry for his actions
it's illegal he is sorry

I will reach out
right out to say it's all right
it's all right
it's all right
he is turning his face away
I have waved at him and seen him wave
he was sad about his actions
we have waved them all away
he is small
he is tiny
he has gone away

> *MR D wanders out. THE DAUGHTER emerges, and looks in the same window-pane he was looking in.*

THE DAUGHTER
I wish I had a friend
I wish I had a friend in the mirror
and I'd say to her
I'd say to her:
you're just the same as me!
you're just the same as me

let's never me and you get old
let's never me and you forget
each other's face!
let's never me and you get old
let's never me and you forget
each other's face
let's never me and you
forget

> *MR D returns and sees her. He sings 'Happy Birthday' but can only recall the melody of its first line.*

MR D
happy birthday to you
happy birthday to you

THE DAUGHTER
It's not my birthday
it's not

MR D
happy birthday to you
happy birthday to you

THE DAUGHTER
It's not my birthday
not my birthday

    MR D advances on her, arms outstretched.

MR D
happy birthday to you
happy birthday to you

    THE DAUGHTER flees in terror.

    THE CAREGIVER arrives, too late to know that her DAUGHTER is the cause of MR D's anxiety.

> **THE CAREGIVER**
> What a clever one you are
> you know it's your birthday!
> you heard us talking
> you remember your birthday!
> we've planned a party
> oh I hope you're ready
> what a clever one you are
> you know it's your birthday!

MR D
over the garden
I am walking to see her
that's how I come

> **THE CAREGIVER**
> You do love a garden

on the pink rose pathway
I look at my present
I stop for a time

> you do love your roses

it's cloudy outside
as I wrap my present
where is my present?

                              what did you bring her?

it is given already
I gave her the present

                                  she has it already?

carried upstairs
there was lightning and thunder
and there
there were snowdrops

                              it's just like today then!

when her back was turning
she gathered my present
up in a staircase

                              she carried your present

there go the stairs
away where she went
and around, around

                              she might be a time then

I'll come with my present
sun in the cloud
of magnolia paper

                                  what did you just say?
                                  what did you just say?
                                  what did you bring her

just what she wanted

                                  what did you bring her
                            that was just what she wanted
                                  what did you bring her
                                  she'd always remember?
                                  what did you bring her
                            through lightning and thunder?
                        what did you wrap in magnolia paper?
                                  what did you bring her

that made her so happy?
what did you bring her
through lightning and thunder?
what did you bring her
that was just – what?

just what she wanted

MR D goes quiet. THE CAREGIVER goes.

VOICES OF BOYS
at the end of the day
till the end of the day
at the end of the day
till the end of the day

MRS D is speaking on the phone.

MRS D
You haven't been for ages
of course he wonders why
you are his family
at the end of the day

VOICES OF BOYS
at the end of the day
till the end of the day
at the end of the day
till the end of the day

THE CAREGIVER is arguing with her DAUGHTER.

THE CAREGIVER
What shall I do with you?
you'll be the death of me
and I can't take you home
till the end of the day

THE DAUGHTER
Nothing happened mummy
I've been here all the time
it's going to snow forever
snow till the end of day

VOICES OF BOYS
at the end of the day
till the end of the day
at the end of the day
till the end of the day

THE CLINICIAN-SCIENTIST
To recognise
to honour
to appreciate
to change
to stay the course
regardless

VOICES OF BOYS
at the end of the day
till the end of the day
at the end of the day
till the end of the day

END OF ACT ONE.

ACT TWO

MR D has wrapped everything around him – the photograph album, a plate, a plastic cup – in newspaper. He clutches one wrapped present to him.

MR D
I have had the most terrible news
from the doctor who's my doctor

I have had most terrible news
I will fold here in the chair for me

they send a different doctor

I wait for the yellow warm to grow

they send two kind old ladies
with pictures of me in a book
and pictures of me on a page

they smile at me I'm in the sand

the yellow warm is old

then the dead river through the room
the blue hush
hush it's after

I am ready for the doctor's news
I will be told today

two ladies and one different doctor

I think sometimes no one who ever
comes here ever
comes again

THE CAREGIVER comes, unwrapping everything. But he clutches the one present, and she lets him keep it. MRS D comes, THE CAREGIVER goes.

MR D
are you –
are you?

over the garden
I'm walking to see her

MRS D
Why should I listen?

that's how I come
on the pink rose pathway
I look at my present

Why should I listen?

I stop for a time
it is cloudy outside
as I wrap my present

I haven't a present

you haven't a present
it isn't your birthday
when is your birthday

Perhaps I don't have one

stairs, there are stars!
stairs
going up in the sky
there is lightning!

No there is no lightning

you missed it!
lightning and thunder
thunder and round
and round there's thunder

No there's no thunder!

where is the staircase?
where is the girl
I have got her a present

The Birthday Girl

magnolia paper...
magnolia paper,
magnolia paper!

Just what a girl wants

magnolia paper
snow on the stairs

Just what a girl wants

she is smiling and smiling

Vanishing vanishing

just what she wanted

A vanishing girl
on a vanishing staircase
why must I listen
to nothing that happened?
Where are you now
who was all that I wanted?
Where are you now
who could make me so happy?
Why do I listen
to nothing that happened?
Where are you now
who was all that I wanted?
Where are you now
who could make me so –

MRS D, spent from sorrow, relents and softens.

MRS D
O now I remember
now I see her
I see her
opening presents
a garden, a staircase...
You *said* she was there

You know her so well

MR D
it was just what she wanted

it was just what she wanted
I tied it with ribbons

are you her grandmother?

MRS D flinches. She rises, and starts to take her leave of him. At the door she looks back. He is still waiting for an answer. She nods once. Then she nods a few times – there is nothing to be done – and she leaves.

Her mobile rings.

MRS D
Dear?

Dear...
of course he knows his children
he may not always seem to
he may not always say, he may not
say a word
not a word
dear...

dear...
I know it's just a birthday
but it's your father's birthday, O
we tried to make it jolly
he got so cross
dear...

the doctors come with clipboards
they want to know what birthdays mean
to him – without his loving sons
what *do* they mean,
dear?

Dear?

MRS D goes away.

THE DAUGHTER creeps into MR D's room, and sees him with his wrapped present.

MR D sees her. He stands up and holds out the present to her.

MR D

happy birthday to you
happy birthday to you

She takes the present and puts it back on the table.

MR D stares at it. He picks it up and holds it out to her again. Again, when he sings 'Happy Birthday' he knows only the melody of the first line. She tries to teach him the rest.

MR D

happy birthday to you
happy birthday to you

                                            THE DAUGHTER
                                            Happy birthday to you

happy birthday to you

                                            happy birthday *dear* – ?
                                            happy birthday *dear* – ?

She takes the present again and puts it back on the table.

                                            THE DAUGHTER
                                            happy birthday *dear* – ?

MR D picks it up and holds it out to her a third time.

MR D

happy birthday to you!
happy birthday to you!

She grabs the present and runs out of the room. He walks to the door, confused.

MR D

happy birthday to you

She comes in from the opposite direction, stifling laughter, puts the present on the table again and runs away. He is looking in the wrong direction. When he turns he sees the present. He looks at it without understanding. He goes back to his chair, picks up the present and clutches it to him. He rocks in his chair.

She creeps back again, fascinated.

MR D sees her, stands up and holds the present out to her.

MR D
happy birthday to you!
happy birthday to you!

THE DAUGHTER
What??

happy birthday to you!
happy birthday to you!

What you give me this for?
What for?

Happy birthday to you!
Happy birthday to you!

Give a present to my mum,
she likes you more than me!
You don't know who my mum is
and you don't know me!
You don't know me!

She throws the present and the wrapping on the floor.

THE DAUGHTER
You don't know me!

MR D is distraught, and tries to pick it up.

THE DAUGHTER
Why do you care so much about it?
it's nothing, it's all right
you don't know me from anyone
it's nothing, it's all right

*THE CAREGIVER, MRS D and THE CLINICIAN-SCIENTIST are approaching
fast. It is too late to get back to her store-room! She steps into a tiny alcove
and hides there.*

MR D
it's nothing
it's all right
all right

VOICES OF BOYS
at end o the day
is time o is time o
want o go o
will o be away

go o way
way away

MR D points towards the alcove.

MR D
she's right behind the tree
right there!
this way! no...
that way! no
right there!

THE CAREGIVER, THE CLINICIAN-SCIENTIST and MRS D arrive in the room.

MR D	**CAREGIVER/CLINICIAN-SCIENTIST/MRS D**
there!	There is no one
she's right behind the tree!	there is no one
right there!	there is no one there
	there is no one there
she doesn't mean it	there is no one
she's right behind...	

THE DAUGHTER sings in her hiding place.

THE DAUGHTER
(There is no one
no one no one no one
no one there
no one here)

MR D	**CAREGIVER/CLINICIAN-SCIENTIST/MRS D**
behind the tree	there is no one there
she's right behind	no one there
the tree the tree	no one there
right there	no one there
the tree	no one there no no
she doesn't mean it	no one here
doesn't mean it	no one there

THE CAREGIVER
You unwrapped your present
you spoiled the surprise

MRS D
Spoiled the surprise!

THE DAUGHTER
(Spoiled the surprise!)

MR D
she doesn't mean it
I know where's she's hiding
right there!

THE CAREGIVER
There?!

THE CLINICIAN-SCIENTIST
Look
look
look where he says
look so he can see you looking
what's true for him is true
it is true now, in the room!

MRS D
There?!

MR D
the birthday girl!

> *THE CAREGIVER looks in the alcove, expecting no one, but sees her DAUGHTER. She is horrified – she would lose her job! She turns back.*

THE CAREGIVER
No one!
No one there!

MRS D
No one there

THE DAUGHTER
(No one there)

MR D
the birthday girl
we went to the fairground
we had green tickets
in rolls of tickets
she's right there!

CAREGIVER/DAUGHTER/MRS D
There is no one
there is no one there

MR D
the birthday girl!

CAREGIVER/DAUGHTER/MRS D
There is no one
there is no one there
no one

MR D
she's right behind the tree

THE CAREGIVER
Never was
never will be
no need to look in there

DAUGHTER/MRS D
No need to look

MR D
the tree
she's hiding

THE CLINICIAN-SCIENTIST
A very good place to look

MRS D
There?

THE CLINICIAN-SCIENTIST
But she's hiding somewhere else, my friend

THE DAUGHTER
(Here!)

CAREGIVER/DAUGHTER/MRS D
No one there
there is no one
no one

Never was
never will be

No one there
will be
no one there

MRS D
I'm not even there
I'm wiped from this picture
I never saw the fairground
I never had a birthday

THE CLINICIAN-SCIENTIST
All of it is him
all he's ever been
everything he is
has been
is still
shall be
he's shedding light on everything

MRS D
For me? Light for me?
I never knew this schoolboy
there was a nice young man I knew
I never knew this child
this special man you came to study
this case
shedding light on everything

but me
everyone but me

THE CLINICIAN-SCIENTIST
What he believes is true
we have to make-believe
we have to make-believe

THE CAREGIVER *(For her Daughter to hear.)*
How can I say you're there?
no one knows you're there

THE DAUGHTER
(Hide and seek
hide and seek
no one knows I'm here)

CAREGIVER/DAUGHTER	**MRS D**
We have to make	I cannot make
have to make believe	cannot make believe
we have to make	I cannot make
have to make believe	cannot make believe
make believe	make believe
make believe	make believe

MR D
she's right behind the tree!
right there!

CAREGIVER/DAUGHTER/MRS D
There's no one no one
never was
never will be
never will be
never will be

MRS D/DAUGHTER
No one will be!

    MR D talks to himself. MRS D addresses THE CLINICIAN-SCIENTIST.

MR D	**MRS D**
She is right behind all right	Young man, dear man
she says I'll be invited	write in your book of light
it isn't	take note
isn't on a school day	note well
they send two kind old ladies	he was once a sharp young man
with pictures of me in a book	the brightest gentleman
they smile at me	I love what's left of him
I'm in the sand	I love what's left of him
	I loved the flowers
	buried in the snow
why have you gone away?	
you always go away	
	write in your book of light
	his wife is left behind
	waving like a daughter
who are you?	and write
	she loved what remained
mrs white I miss you	
	and wished she could come with him
	on business far away
	catch the light he sheds
mrs light I miss u	catch the light he sheds
	dear man, young man
	write the book of light
	lift it in the sunshine
	but leave me here alone
	leave us here alone
	to meet once again
	to part once again
	meet again
	part once again

THE CLINICIAN-SCIENTIST closes his notebook and politely takes his leave of MR D. He indicates for THE CAREGIVER also to withdraw, which she does, with a last exasperated, helpless look at where her DAUGHTER is hiding. MR and MRS D are left alone.

MR D
no one who ever
comes
here comes again

> **VOICES OF BOYS**
> *at the end of the day*
> *when it's time and it's time to*
> *you will want to go home*
> *you will be home anyway*

THE CLINICIAN-SCIENTIST, though he has left MR and MRS D, reopens his notebook, and continues to think about the case.

THE CLINICIAN-SCIENTIST
You have to make believe
you have to make believe
there is a world he sees

sometimes I see a world beyond
beyond this long disease
sometimes I see a world beyond
a world beyond
this long disease

> **VOICES OF BOYS**
> *A world beyond*

MRS D departs from her husband.

MR D closes his eyes.

On the screen, again a still picture comes to life, a class photograph, all are singing. We move slowly along the rows of boys standing at the back...Then once again we see images from the party, but this time they run rapidly backwards – the present abandoned in the mud – the hands tearing wrapping off – the tree someone is hiding behind – the see-saws and swings all moving in the rain – the garden with roses – the grand circular staircase – the door of the big house, the door opening slowly – the picture fades to black.

At last THE DAUGHTER *thinks the coast is clear, and emerges from the alcove, to see* MR D, *apparently asleep, once again clutching the wrapped present to his chest.*

THE DAUGHTER
I have to make believe
just like they told me to!
what he believes is true
they said
for him it's true

it's like the world for him
is like some other world!
it's like some other world, O...
what he believes is true for him...
true! O

I'm visiting his planet
I'm the Birthday Girl

MR D wakes and sees her.

THE DAUGHTER *(A whisper to him.)*
I am the Birthday Girl...
I'm the Birthday Girl!

MR D rises, holding the present out to her once again.

MR D
over the garden I've come to see you

She takes the present from him and starts unwrapping it gently.

MR D
sun in the cloud of magnolia paper

She admires the wrapping paper.

MR D
we went to the fair we had green tickets

She smiles and nods as if it were true.

MR D
I tied it with ribbons

She opens the present.

MR D
just what you always wanted

THE DAUGHTER
Just what I always wanted!
Just what I always wanted...

She clutches the present to her, and slowly retreats from the room, waving goodbye to him and smiling.

THE DAUGHTER
Just what I always wanted
always wanted

He waves to her as she goes.

MR D hums happily to himself. For the first time he is singing.

VOICES OF BOYS
I A O A
is I O is I O
O oo O O
E A O
E A O
A is I O
is I O
I A O A is A

Now he wears a beatific smile.

On the screen we see the class photograph come to life again, we move along the row of seated girls...flashes of fairground rides, a sunny day, two hands hand-in-hand... The row of girls at the very front, all seated on the ground... The whirl of a fairground ride, her hair blowing right beside him... To the last girl in the line, a pretty girl with an alice-band just like the Daughter's – the Birthday Girl.

The picture fades.

MR D is still looking at where she went. Then he is looking at the snow falling through the orange street-lamps in the twilight. He returns to his chair. He is still smiling happily. Very, very slowly, the smile fades as the memory fades. He is looking straight ahead. He has no expression.

Fade to darkness.

END.